PILAR CUDER DOMINGUEZ • RAQUEL RODRIGUEZ T
DAVID SPENCER • DAVID VAUGHAN

Teamwork

RESOURCE PACK

2

Dear Teachers,

We are very pleased that you are interested in using this *Teamwork Resource Pack*.

While writing the activities for the *Teamwork Resource Pack*, we had in mind the secondary students we have taught over the years. Although teaching in secondary schools can be very enjoyable and satisfying, we are also aware of the problems involved, in particular that of mixed ability within the same group.

Using these photocopiable activities, we are offering you the flexibility to deal with the mixed abilities that will inevitably exist among your students. The Pack is divided into units which follow the order of the units in *Teamwork Student's Book*, and each unit is organized in the following way:

Class Activities – these are communicative activities designed for oral interaction. Each activity has accompanying teaching notes on the reverse, where the aim of the activity and type of interaction (groupwork, pairwork, etc) is specified, together with an indication of the target language and timing. This is followed by detailed suggestions for procedure. Beside *Activity* you will note that there is always an (R) or an (E); this indicates whether the activity is intended as reinforcement or extension of the content of the corresponding unit in the Student's Book.

Revision and Extension – within any class we have found that there are usually two or three students who find the work very difficult and who have trouble in keeping up with the others. On the other hand, there are sometimes one or two students who find everything easy and who feel they are not being challenged enough. These activities are designed to provide extra material for those individual students to do alone, according to their specific needs. There is an answer key for these activities at the end of the *Resource Pack*.

We hope that you find this *Teamwork Resource Pack* useful and that you and your students enjoy the activities.

Pilar Cuder Domínguez
Raquel Rodríguez Tuñas

1 *Team Up!*

11 15 13 12 17

Name	Age

981 4326

Name	Telephone Number

English history art maths

Name	Favourite School Subject

Name	Hobby

TEAM UP! REPORT

Name	Age	Telephone Number	Favourite School Subject	Hobby

Written by Pilar Cuder Domínguez, Raquel Rodríguez Tuñas
© David Spencer, David Vaughan 1996 Published by Heinemann English Language Teaching

1 Team Up!

· · · · · · · · · · · · · · · · ·

Activity   (R) Asking for and giving personal information

Language   **Personal information**

Interaction **Groups of 4**

Time   **20 minutes**

1 Make copies of the worksheet for each group.

2 Ask students to get into groups of four and give them the material. Ask each group to appoint a secretary.

3 Ask the students to divide the worksheet up into five different sections and take one section each. The secretary takes the *Team Up! Report* chart, too.

4 Each student is responsible for finding out one piece of information by asking the others in the group. For example, student A finds out the age of the others, student B finds out their phone numbers, student C finds out their favourite school subject, etc.

5 When each member of the group has completed their chart, the secretary asks each student to report their findings and puts the information together in the group chart.

6 When they have finished, they can display the results around the classroom walls.

2 Summer's over!

_____ 's summer holidays

Good/bad?	😃	☐	😐	☐	🙁	☐
Where? (go…/stay…)	⛰️	☐	🏖️	☐	🏙️	☐
Who with?	🎒	☐	👨‍👩‍👧	☐	👨‍👩‍👧	☐
When?	JULY	☐	AUG	☐	SEPT	☐
How long?	S M T W Th F S	☐	(calendar)	☐	(calendar)	☐

✂️ -

3 Find someone who ...

Name

stayed at home _____

went to a summer camp _____

visited another country _____

practised English _____

made a new friend _____

travelled by plane _____

watched a new film _____

was bored in the summer _____

did a lot of sport _____

played computer games _____

Written by Pilar Cuder Domínguez, Raquel Rodríguez Tuñas
© David Spencer, David Vaughan 1996 Published by Heinemann English Language Teaching

Photocopiable   **5**

2 Summer's over!

· · · · · · · · · · · · · · · · · · · ·

Activity (R) Talking about summer holidays

Language Past simple

Interaction Pairs

Time 30 minutes

1 Make a copy of the worksheet for each student.

2 Make sure the students know the language corresponding to the pictures and if necessary revise the question forms.

3 Students work in pairs. First they complete the top of the chart with their partner's name. Then in turns they ask questions and tick the corresponding answer box.

4 When the pairs have finished, they exchange the completed charts with another pair. Each pair writes two short paragraphs about the other pair, using the information they have been given.

5 Finally, ask some of the students to read out their texts. Correct with the whole class.

3 Find someone who ...

· ·

Activity (E) Talking about summer holidays

Language Past simple

Interaction Mingle (2 mini-mingles)

Time 25 minutes

1 Make one copy of the worksheet for each student.

2 Divide the class into two groups and send them to opposite ends of the classroom.

3 The aim is to find classmates who answer 'yes' to the questions and write their names on the corresponding line.

1 You name it!

Match the words and the pictures.

boardrubber   pencil
blackboard   notebook   chalk
ruler   desk   dictionary

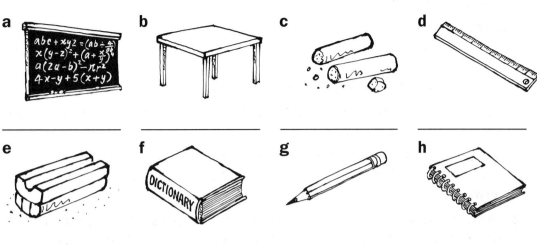

a _____   b _____   c _____   d _____

e _____   f _____   g _____   h _____

2 Welcome back!

▶ **A** *David is talking about his holiday with Sally. Match Sally's questions and David's answers.*

1 Did you have a good holiday?   a To France.
2 Where did you go?   b On 31st August.
3 Did you go with your family?   c Um, travelled around, swam in
                                          the pool.
4 What did you do?   d Yes, all right.
5 When did you come back?   e Yes, with my parents.

▶ **B** *Sally is talking to a friend about David's summer. Complete the dialogue.*

a __Did__ David __have__ a good holiday?
   Yes, it _____ all right.

b Where _____ he ____?
   He _____ to France.

c _____ with ____ family?
   Yes, he _____ with ____ parents.

d What _____?
   He _____ around, and he _____ in the pool.

e When _____ back?
   He _____ on 31st August.

Written by Pilar Cuder Domínguez, Raquel Rodríguez Tuñas
© David Spencer, David Vaughan 1996 Published by Heinemann English Language Teaching

1 Check your spelling!

a *esptro*

_____

b *rbklaocbda*

_____

c **rbedabrorub**

_____

d **kbeontoo**

_____

e yniictorad

_____

f hlakc

_____

g *ruomctep*

_____

h *errlu*

_____

i krcaucsk

_____

2 Dear Peggy Sue

▶ *Complete this letter.*

Dear Peggy Sue,

I hope you had a good summer. I had a great time! I went

to _____ with my _____. We took

the _____. We _____ to a place

called Brighton. The weather was _____ – it didn't

_____ once! So we _____ and

_____ every day. We _____

a lot of photos. I'll send you some. Tomorrow is the first day back

at school. Summer is over!

Write soon.

Love,

_____

Written by Pilar Cuder Domínguez, Raquel Rodríguez Tuñas
© David Spencer, David Vaughan 1996 Published by Heinemann English Language Teaching

1 *Talking about magazines*

	Partner 1	Partner 2
a Do you like magazines?	_____	_____
b What is your favourite magazine?	_____	_____
c Do you buy magazines?	_____	_____
d Where do you read magazines?	_____	_____
e When do you read magazines?	_____	_____
f What is your favourite section?	_____	_____

✂ -

2 *Top ten*

	GUESSES	ANSWERS
think / brilliant		
like		
don't mind		
don't enjoy		
think / awful		

How **well** do you know your partner? Check your score!

5 points = extremely well
4 points = very well
3 points = quite
2 points = not very well
1 point = very little
0 points = not at all!

Written by Pilar Cuder Domínguez, Raquel Rodríguez Tuñas
© David Spencer, David Vaughan 1996 Published by Heinemann English Language Teaching

1 Talking about magazines

Activity (R) Talking about likes and habits

Language Present simple

Interaction Groups of 3

Time 20 minutes

1 Make one copy of the worksheet for each student.

2 Ask students to form groups of three.

3 Students take turns to ask and answer questions to complete their charts. If necessary, practise the pronunciation of the questions with the whole class before they start.

4 Some groups tell the rest of the class their results.

2 Top ten

Activity (R) Talking about likes and dislikes

Language Simple present

Interaction Pairs

Time 15 minutes

1 Make one copy of the worksheet for each student.

2 Ask students to get into pairs.

3 In pairs, students agree on two other musicians and complete the records with their names, but warn them not to show their opinions of these people.
If they like, students can use local groups.

4 Individually, students complete the GUESSES column, trying to guess their partners' likes and dislikes by writing the name of a musician next to each category.

5 In pairs, students ask questions to find out if they have guessed correctly. They complete the ANSWERS column with the correct answers.

Example:
Student 1: *What do you think of Bach?*
Student 2: *I think he's brilliant!*

6 When they have finished, they check how well they know each other by looking at the key.

3 Dominoes

3 Dominoes

· · · · · · · · · · · · · · · ·

Activity   **(E) Talking about likes and dislikes**

Language   **Present simple**

Interaction **Groups of any number**

Time   **20 minutes**

1 Make a copy of the worksheet for each group.

2 Get students into groups and ask them to cut up the cards.

3 One student starts by placing a card on the table. He/she says a sentence using both pictures on the card. The next student puts down another card that has one picture which is the same, and then says an appropriate sentence.

Example:
Student 1: *I like swimming but I hate skateboarding.*
Student 2: *I love skateboarding and I like cooking, too.*

4 The game continues like this until all the cards have been used.

1 As different as chalk and cheese

► *Complete this chart with free time activities.*

	ME	**MY BEST FRIEND**	**MY PARENTS**
LOVE			
HATE			
DON'T MIND			
ENJOY			

Now write a short paragraph using the information in the chart. Use <u>and</u> and <u>but</u> to link the sentences, when necessary.

For example: I love reading comics but my parents love reading
                         newspapers.

2 At the newsagent's

► *Match the magazines and your opinions and write six true sentences about your likes and dislikes.*

a _____

b _____

c _____

d _____

e _____

f _____

Written by Pilar Cuder Domínguez, Raquel Rodríguez Tuñas
© David Spencer, David Vaughan 1996 Published by Heinemann English Language Teaching

1 Which section?

▶ Match the magazine extracts with the words in the box below.

d | **BBC1** **13.40:** The World Today, **14.25:** Film: Dracula, **16.50:** The Prince of Bel Air.

a A romantic situation in your future. There's an element of danger.

e The new James Bond film *Black Eye* opened in London yesterday, with Tina Turner leading the

b **across:** wild animal
down: Popular British magazine

c **New Golf Project**

Marbella is going to have seven more golf courses. Mr Ballesteros, the golf professional living in the south

f How do you see your future, Princess Dina? I'm not sure. The situation at present is awful. Why did you marry James? I was in love with him.

| crossword | sport | film review | horoscope | TV guide | interview |

a _____   d _____

b _____   e _____

c _____   f _____

2 Competition winner!

▶ Imagine you are going to interview the winner of this month's Mega competition from TEAM UP! magazine. Prepare some questions for the interview.

a _____?
  (place and date of birth)

b _____?
  (likes & dislikes)

c _____?
  (hobbies)

d _____?
  (favourite food/drink)

e _____?
  (family)

f _____?
  (pets)

Written by Pilar Cuder Domínguez, Raquel Rodríguez Tuñas
© David Spencer, David Vaughan 1996 Published by Heinemann English Language Teaching

1 The perfect job!

	Like	Don't mind	Hate
beautiful clothes	_____	_____	_____
long distances	_____	_____	_____
a computer	_____	_____	_____
a uniform	_____	_____	_____
danger	_____	_____	_____
new people	_____	_____	_____
in a team	_____	_____	_____
at a desk all day	_____	_____	_____
outside	_____	_____	_____
in hotels	_____	_____	_____

✂ ---

2 My inner life

How often ... ?		Key	How often ... ?		Key
	cry			feel sad	
	need to be alone			write love poems	
	fall in love			write a diary	
	daydream			tell your secrets	

Key:

1 = never	3 = usually	5 = once a month
2 = sometimes	4 = often	6 = twice a year

Written by Pilar Cuder Domínguez, Raquel Rodríguez Tuñas
© David Spencer, David Vaughan 1996 Published by Heinemann English Language Teaching

1 The perfect job!

••••••••••••••••••••••••

Activity   **(R) Talking about likes and dislikes**

Language   **Present simple**

Interaction **Pairs and groups**

Time   **20–30 minutes**

1 Make one copy of the worksheet for each student.

2 Ask students to get into pairs.

3 Students ask and answer questions and complete their charts.

    Before they start, make sure students know what verb to use in each question: **wearing** beautiful clothes, **travelling** long distances, **using** a computer, **staying** in hotels etc.

    Example:
    Student A: *Do you like wearing beautiful clothes?*
    Student B: *Yes, I love it!*

4 When they have completed the chart, ask students to get into groups of four or five.

5 Each student reports to the group and they all try to find the perfect job for each member.

6 One member of each group reports to the rest of the class.

    Example:
    A pilot is the perfect job for Anna because she likes travelling long distances, sleeping in hotels, and wearing a uniform.

2 My inner life

••••••••••••••••••••

Activity   **(R) Talking about feelings**

Language   **Present simple**

Interaction **Pairs**

Time   **15 minutes**

1 Make one copy of the worksheet for each student.

2 Get students into pairs. Ask students to read the question prompts and make sure they understand them.

3 Students take turns to ask and answer questions and write the corresponding number of their partner's answer in the Key column.

    Example:
    Student A: *How often do you cry?*
    Student B: *Sometimes.* (Student A writes *2* in the Key column.)

3 *What's my line?*

ZOO KEEPER
dangerous job
love animals

work in a zoo

PARK KEEPER
favourite season: spring
meet many people

open park at 8 am

MODEL
exciting job
fly long distances

love wearing beautiful clothes

PILOT
dangerous job
wear a uniform

fly long distances

FOOTBALLER
rich and popular
work on Sundays

love sports

BUS DRIVER
sit all day
hate traffic

love driving

MUSIC SHOP ASSISTANT
stand all day
love music

have many CDs and tapes

FILM ACTOR
rich and famous
meet many people

love cameras

Written by Pilar Cuder Domínguez, Raquel Rodríguez Tuñas
© David Spencer, David Vaughan 1996 Published by Heinemann English Language Teaching

3 What's my line?

· ·

Activity　　(E) Talking about jobs

Language　　**Present simple**

Interaction　**Groups of 4**

Time　　　　**15–30 minutes**

1 Make a copy of the material for each group.

2 Ask students to form groups of four and cut up the cards – without looking at them!

3 They shuffle the cards, face down, and each takes two cards. It doesn't matter if there are groups with fewer students; each student takes only two cards, and the remaining cards will not be used.

4 Each student turns over the two cards and fills in the blank on each card with an activity connected to the job.

5 One student starts by giving clues from the card about his/her job. The other students can ask him/her questions, and the first person to guess continues the game.

Example:
Student 1: *My job is quite dangerous.*
Student 2: *Do you have to fly long distances?*
Student 1: *No, I don't. I don't travel in my job.*
etc.

6 Once they have used up one card, they continue by role playing the other job.

1 What a life!

▶ A *Read the article about Judith Taylor on page 16 of Teamwork Student's Book 2, and complete the chart below.*

How often?	Once a week	Twice a week	Three or four times a week	Once a month	Not very often
Activity					

▶ B *Now write a short article using this information.*

Judith Taylor has a busy life. Once a week, she ...

_____

_____

_____

_____

_____

2 Super models

▶ *You work for a fashion magazine and you're looking for a new model. Compare these two models using the words in the box below.*

A   B

Claudia Sniff   Cindy Crowfeet

> thin   tall   beautiful
> short   elegant

Claudia is taller than Cindy.

_____

_____

_____

_____

Written by Pilar Cuder Domínguez, Raquel Rodríguez Tuñas
© David Spencer, David Vaughan 1996 Published by Heinemann English Language Teaching

Photocopiable   19

1 That's life!

▶ **A** *Read the text about Judith Taylor on page 16 of Teamwork Student's Book 2 again and complete the box below.*

Advantages	Disadvantages

▶ **B** *Now write a paragraph about her life. Use <u>although, so, and, because, or</u> to link your sentences.*

Judith's life is exciting although … _____

_____

_____

_____

_____

_____

_____

_____

_____

_____

1 *Are you healthy?*

1 How many pieces of fruit do you eat every day?

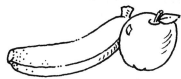

Name	a one	b two	c more

2 How much water do you drink every day?

Name	a one litre	b two litres	c more

3 How often do you eat fast food?

Name	a very often	b once a week	c once a month

4 How many sit-ups can you do in a minute?

Name	a one	b ten	c more

Group results		Total (b + c)	Group results		Total (b + c)
1	b = c =		3	b = c =	
2	b = c =		4	b = c =	

Score
a = 0 points
b = 1 point
c = 2 points

Written by Pilar Cuder Domínguez, Raquel Rodríguez Tuñas
© David Spencer, David Vaughan 1996 Published by Heinemann English Language Teaching

1 Are you healthy?

· ·

Activity   (R) Talking about health and fitness

Language   Present simple

Interaction Groups of 4

Time   25 minutes

1 Make one copy of the worksheet for each group.

2 Get students to form groups of four and ask them to choose a secretary for the group. If there are fewer in the group, students can choose which question each wants to ask, and leave out any extra ones.

3 Each student asks his/her question to everyone in the group and ticks the appropriate answer column on the chart.

4 When they have finished asking the questions, the secretary takes the GROUP RESULTS chart and asks the other students in the group for the results. Then he/she notes down the number of points scored per answer, using the key, and completes the TOTAL column.

5 Finally, different groups compare their results to find out which is the healthiest group in the class.

Sports special!

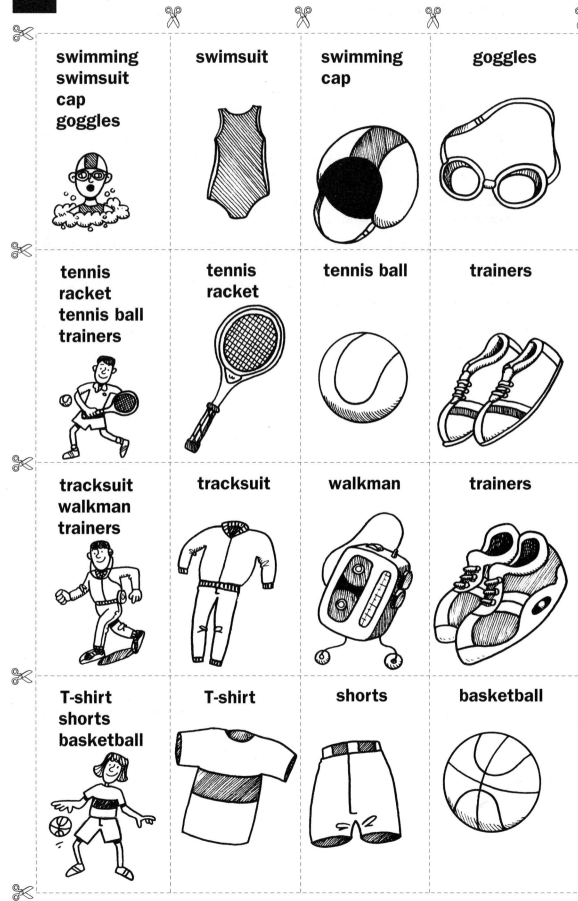

swimming swimsuit cap goggles	swimsuit	swimming cap	goggles
tennis racket tennis ball trainers	tennis racket	tennis ball	trainers
tracksuit walkman trainers	tracksuit	walkman	trainers
T-shirt shorts basketball	T-shirt	shorts	basketball

Written by Pilar Cuder Domínguez, Raquel Rodríguez Tuñas
© David Spencer, David Vaughan 1996 Published by Heinemann English Language Teaching

Photocopiable **23**

2 Sports special!

· ·

Activity   (R) Talking about sports

Language   *go* and *play* for sports; requests

Interaction   Groups of 4

Time   15–20 minutes

1   Make one copy of the material for each group.

2   Students get into groups of four. Ask them to cut out the cards.

3   Each student in the group takes a master card (the card that has the sport and the three items needed). They shuffle the other cards and take three each.

4   The aim is to get all three cards related to a sport. To do so, they have to ask questions to the student on their right.

    Example:

    Student 1: *I want to go swimming. Can I have a swimsuit?*

    Student 2: *Yes, of course. Here you are. / I'm sorry. I haven't got a swimsuit.*

    If the student receives the answer 'yes', then he or she can take that card. If the answer is 'no', it is the next student's turn.

5   The winner is the first student to complete the set.

3 *On the phone*

Student A

Part 1
You phone Susan
at 6 pm on Monday.

Part 2
The phone rings
at 4 pm on Thursday.

- Hello. It's_____ here. Can I speak to Susan?
- Oh, really? Who with?
- Does she always _____ on Monday?
- How long _____?
- No, thanks. Bye-bye!

- 428 1049
- Sorry he's not in. He's _____.
- With _____.
- Yes, he does.
- Well, he finishes at_____. _____ a message?
- Bye!

After school activities				
Mondays & Thursdays	Susan	Mark	Jessica	Andrew
4–5 pm	guitar	piano	riding	riding
5–6.30 pm		basketball	cycling	English

Student B

Part 1
The telephone rings
at 6 pm on Monday.

Part 2
Now ring Andrew.
It's 4 pm on Thursday.

- 566 1023
- Sorry, _____ not in. She's _____.
- With _____.
- Yes, she does.
- Well, she finishes at_____. _____ a message?
- Bye!

- Hello. It's _____ here. Can I _____?
- Oh, really? Who with?
- Does he always _____?
- How long _____?
- No, thanks. Bye-bye!

After school activities				
Mondays & Thursdays	Susan	Mark	Jessica	Andrew
4–5 pm	guitar	piano	riding	
5–6.30 pm	basketball	basketball	cycling	English

Written by Pilar Cuder Domínguez, Raquel Rodríguez Tuñas
© David Spencer, David Vaughan 1996 Published by Heinemann English Language Teaching

3 On the phone

· · · · · · · · · · · · · · · · · ·

Activity   (E) Making phone calls

Language   Telephone language; present simple and present continuous

Interaction Pairs

Time   25 minutes

1 Make one copy of the material for each pair.

2 Ask students to get into pairs and give each pair the student A and B material. Ask students to divide the page into two along the dotted line.

3 Explain to students that in the first conversation student A is the caller and B answers the call, and in the second conversation student B is the caller and A answers the phone. Tell them to give their own name when they make the call.

4 To act out the conversation, they use the information in the timetable provided.

1 Goal!

▶ *Write five sentences using the words below.*

a *usually/up/Peter/gets/seven/at*

b *swimming/she/twice/goes/a/week*

c *does/she/every/judo/day*

d *after/play/school/they/football/often*

e *the sports club/my/Mondays/to/on/friends/sometimes/go*

a _____

b _____

c _____

d _____

e _____

2 To be or not to be ... fit!

▶ *Write these activities in the correct column.*

Fit	Unfit

Written by Pilar Cuder Domínguez, Raquel Rodríguez Tuñas
© David Spencer, David Vaughan 1996 Published by Heinemann English Language Teaching

1 Game

▶ *Look at the information below and write a report about this tennis player.*

Name:	Conchita Rodríguez	Pet:	snake ('Wimble')
Born:	1970	Favourite colour:	black
Height:	1,66 m	Hobby:	rugby
Weight:	54 k	Other interests:	cooking
Family:	2 brothers, 1 sister	1992:	Olympics
Special racket:	Wilson Conch	1995:	Wimbledon Champion

_____

_____

_____

_____

_____

_____

_____

_____

2 Then and now

▶ *Who said what? Go back to page 24 in your Student's Book. Match the sentences with the corresponding picture.*

3 I often play outside until bedtime.

4 I have sports lessons five times a week.

5 I have fun at home with my game console.

6 I walk to the cinema.

7 I have sports lessons twice a week.

2 I eat a lot of hamburgers.

1 I have a poster of Michael Jordan.

8 My mother drives me to school.

9 I cycle to school.

A: 3, ... _____

B: _____

Written by Pilar Cuder Domínguez, Raquel Rodríguez Tuñas
© David Spencer, David Vaughan 1996 Published by Heinemann English Language Teaching

1 *The pyramid game*

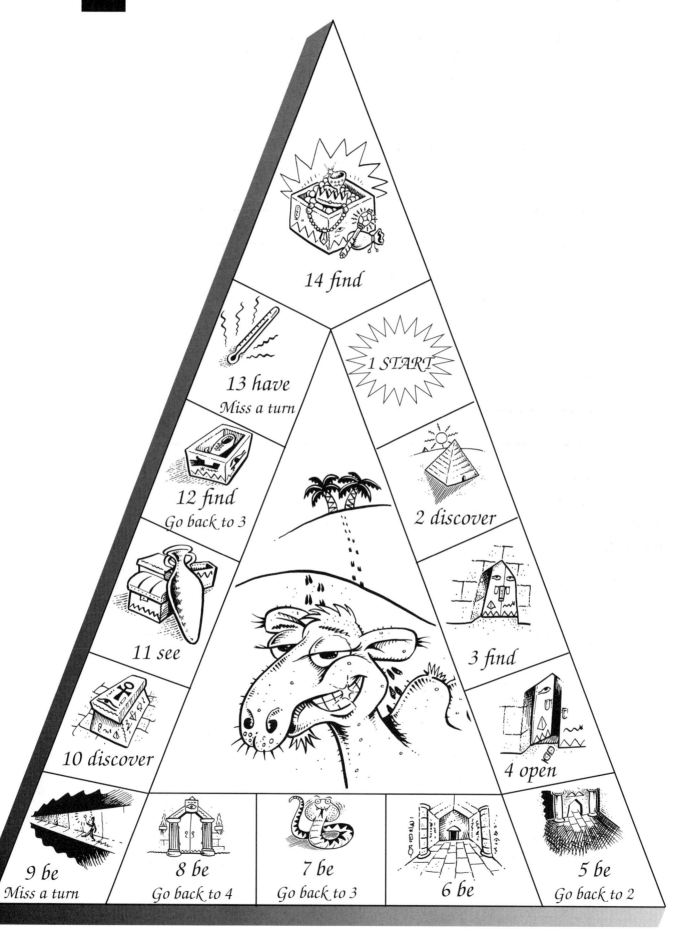

14 find

13 have
Miss a turn

1 START

12 find
Go back to 3

2 discover

11 see

3 find

10 discover

4 open

9 be
Miss a turn

8 be
Go back to 4

7 be
Go back to 3

6 be

5 be
Go back to 2

TEAMWORK RESOURCE PACK 2

Written by Pilar Cuder Domínguez, Raquel Rodríguez Tuñas
© David Spencer, David Vaughan 1996 Published by Heinemann English Language Teaching

1 The pyramid game
· ·

Activity   **(R) Talking about past actions**

Language   **Past simple**

Interaction **Groups (any number)**

Time   **25 minutes**

Preparation: Ask students to bring dice and counters.

---

1 Make one copy of the material for each group. If possible, enlarge it.

2 Tell students they are going to play a board game. The aim of the game is to find the treasure. In turns, they throw the dice and move their counter accordingly.

3 They have to make sentences using the correct past form of the verb in each box. If they can't, they miss a turn.

2 *Lost in the pyramid!*

Student A

There were two tunnels. I took the tunnel on the left. It was very short …

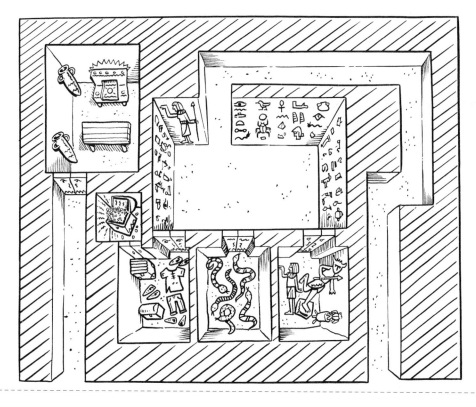

✂ ───

Student B

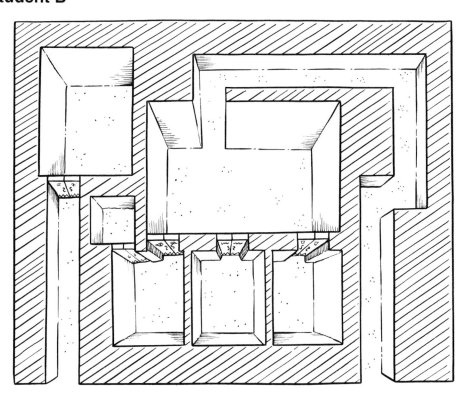

2 Lost in the pyramid

························

Activity   **(E) Finding the way to the treasure**

Language   **Past simple; describing a route**

Interaction **Pairs**

Time   **15 minutes**

1 Make one copy of the worksheet for each pair. Cut up the student A and B material.

2 Ask students to get into pairs and hand out the material.

3 Explain that student A has to describe the route he/she followed to the treasure. Student B has to draw the route and draw a picture, or write the name of the objects mentioned in the appropriate square.

5 Students work in pairs. When they have finished, they compare their worksheets.

6 Finally, students complete student A's text by writing the description of the route.

Suggested text:

There were two tunnels. I took the tunnel on the left. It was very short. I found a door but it was closed. I went back to the entrance and I took the other tunnel. It was very long. At the end of the tunnel I came to a big room with hieroglyphs. There were three doors. I opened the door in the middle and the room was full of snakes. I closed the door. I opened the door on the left. There were many statues. Then I opened the door on the right. There were boxes of shoes and clothes. Next to the boxes there was a little door. When I opened it, I found the treasure.

32 **Photocopiable**
·····················
Written by Pilar Cuder Domínguez, Raquel Rodríguez Tuñas
© David Spencer, David Vaughan 1996 Published by Heinemann English Language Teaching

1 A letter from Egypt

▶ Complete the archaeologist's letter.

I opened the [door]. It was very dark in the tomb,

and I needed my _____. I began to look round the

room. In the middle of the room, there was a _____ and

there were _____, one at each side. Near the bed

I saw two _____. I opened them and they

were full of _____. On the left near the door,

there was a large _____, with

_____ and _____ and wine.

2 A long time ago

▶ Give true answers to these questions using expressions
from the box.

> ... days   ... minutes   ... months   ... years
> ... hours   ... minutes   ... weeks

a *How long ago did you eat pizza?* _____ ago.
b *How long ago did you go shopping?* _____.
c *How long ago did you laugh?* _____.
d *How long ago did you ride a bike?* _____.
e *How long ago did you recycle paper?* _____.
f *How long ago did you watch an exciting film?* _____.

Written by Pilar Cuder Domínguez, Raquel Rodríguez Tuñas
© David Spencer, David Vaughan 1996 Published by Heinemann English Language Teaching

1 Egyptian adventure

▶ *Match the two halves of the sentences.*

1 More than 150 years ago, Conway, Parker and Ben discovered …

2 They found a long tunnel …

3 Ben found a small statue …

4 As soon as Conway and Parker finished their exploration, …

5 On board the *Beatrice* …

6 One night there was a terrible storm …

7 The treasure went to the bottom of the sea and …

a … which went to the heart of the pyramid.

b … they prepared to return to Britain.

c … Ben had a terrible fever and died.

d … a secret pyramid in the Valley of the Kings.

e … and put it in his pocket.

f … Lisa discovered it more than 150 years later.

g … and lightning destroyed the ship.

2 Jumping knights

▶ *Connect the words using the movements of the knight from the game **Chess**, i.e. 2 spaces + 1 space or 1 space + 2 spaces (in any direction except diagonally). Reconstruct the message.*
*Clue: **We opened … .***

 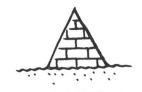

	THE	THE	THE	
IN	FOUND	INCREDIBLE	OPENED	THE
TOMB	HEART	PYRAMID		MOST
	TREASURE	AND	OF	WE

Written by Pilar Cuder Domínguez, Raquel Rodríguez Tuñas
© David Spencer, David Vaughan 1996 Published by Heinemann English Language Teaching

1 Who is X?

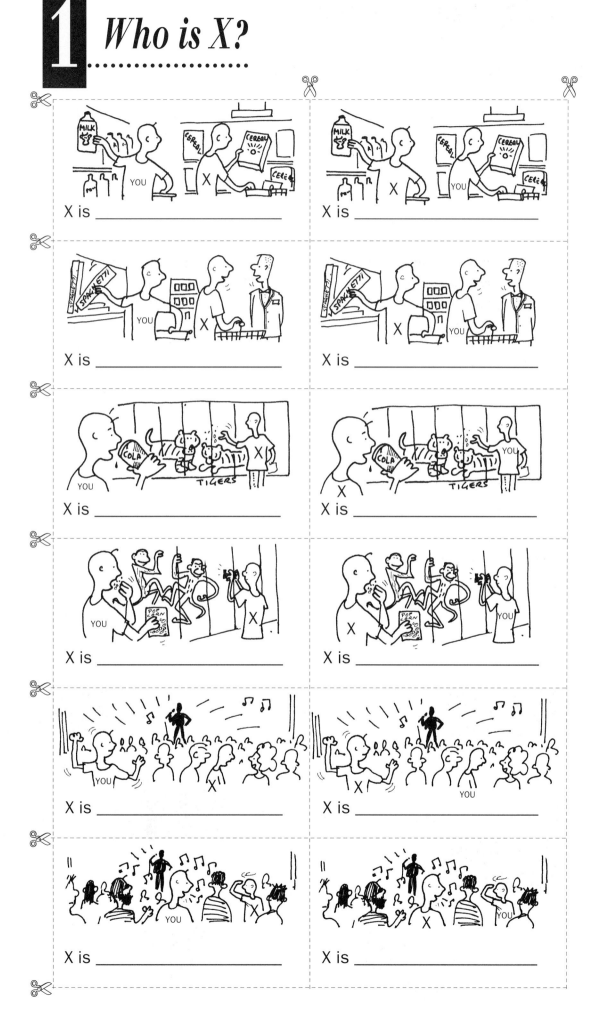

Written by Pilar Cuder Domínguez, Raquel Rodríguez Tuñas
© David Spencer, David Vaughan 1996 Published by Heinemann English Language Teaching

1 Who is X?

· · · · · · · · · · · · · · · · ·

Activity **(R) Talking about past actions in progress**

Language **Past continuous**

Interaction **Mingle (2 mini-mingles)**

Time **25 minutes**

1 Make two copies of the set of role cards for each half of the class with a maximum of twelve students in each group, and cut up the cards. If there are fewer than twelve students in a group, make sure that you take out the two matching cards from the set; you need even numbers in the group. (If necessary, ask two students to work together and share a card).

2 Divide the class into two groups and send them to different parts of the classroom. Give each student a role card.

3 Explain to the students that they saw someone very nice last Saturday night who could be a good friend but they don't know the person (Mr or Ms X). The aim of the activity is to find the person they saw and make friends with him/her.

4 They should take turns to ask and answer questions about last Saturday until they find X. They then write the name of the person in their role cards. With weaker students, you may want to practise possible questions first: Where were you last Saturday night?/ What were you doing there?/ What were you eating/looking at/buying? …

5 When students have found out who X is, they go back to their places.

6 If you think students need further practice, ask them to shuffle the cards and repeat the activity with a different role.

2 *The scene of the crime*

Student A

You are Mrs Black. This is what you saw.
Answer Detective Brown's
questions.

Student B

You are Mr Green. This is what you saw from your window.
Answer Detective Brown's questions.

Student C

You are Mr White. This is what you saw from your window.
Answer Detective Brown's questions.

Student D

You are Detective Brown. Ask the witnesses questions and
complete the chart. Who isn't telling the truth?

	Where?	Weather?	Description of people in street?	What/doing?	What happened?
Mrs Black					
Mr Green					
Mr White					

Written by Pilar Cuder Domínguez, Raquel Rodríguez Tuñas
© David Spencer, David Vaughan 1996 Published by Heinemann English Language Teaching

2 The scene of the crime

· ·

Activity   (E) Describing a scene in the past

Language   Past continuous

Interaction Groups of 4

Time   30 minutes

1 Make one copy of the worksheet for each group of four and ask the students to cut up the cards.

2 Explain to the students that students A, B and C live in the same block of flats in a street where there was a bank robbery. Student D is Detective Brown who is going to interrogate them for details of the scene of the crime. However, one of the students is lying and the detective has to find out who.

3 Student D asks questions using the cues in the chart, first to Mrs Black, then to Mr Green and finally to Mr White, and makes a note of their answers. The students A, B and C answer according to the information they have in their picture. It is important that students do not show each other their pictures.

5 When they finish, student D has to decide who is lying and then report to the class.

3 *The story machine*

Written by Pilar Cuder Domínguez, Raquel Rodríguez Tuñas
© David Spencer, David Vaughan 1996 Published by Heinemann English Language Teaching

3 The story machine

·······························

Activity   (E) Inventing stories

Language   **Past simple; past continuous**

Interaction **Groups of 4–5**

Time   **30 minutes**

1 Make one copy of the material for each group and cut up the cards.

2 Ask students to make groups of four or five.

3 In their groups, they shuffle the cards and put them face down on the desk.

4 Explain to them that the aim of the game is to invent a story. Students take turns to turn over one card and make a sentence with the word or object provided, linking it to the previous sentence so that it makes sense.

5 Finally, ask each group to write their story and then exchange it with another group.

1 Story time

▶ *Look at the pictures and complete the text. Then draw another picture in your notebook and finish the story.*

It was Sunday afternoon. I _____ in the park. The sun _____ and some children _____. I _____ a very boring book.

Suddenly I _____ my friend Jane. She _____ a very long dress, and she _____ across the grass to me. She _____ something in her hand. 'Look, look! I've got two tickets for today's football match. Let's go!' she said.

So we ... _____
_____
_____
_____

2 Interrogation

▶ *Answer these questions.*

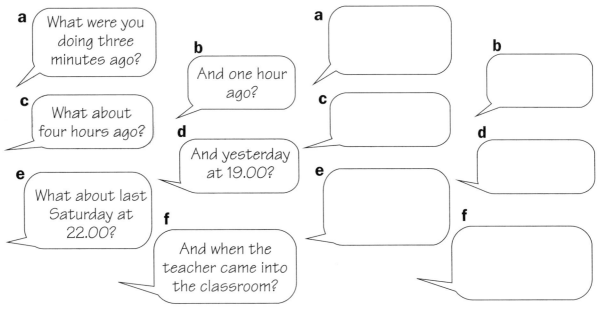

a (What were you doing three minutes ago?)

b (And one hour ago?)

c (What about four hours ago?)

d (And yesterday at 19.00?)

e (What about last Saturday at 22.00?)

f (And when the teacher came into the classroom?)

a
b
c
d
e
f

1 Book puzzle

▶ *What sort of books are these? Match the titles with the extracts.*

Travel Guide to America   The Book of Jokes
The 'BEST' English Dictionary   Collected Poems   Annie's Adventures
The Natural World   Sixteenth-Century America

a
The Indian princess Pocahontas was born in 1595 in Virginia. She made friends with John Smith in 1607. She married John Rolfe in 1614 and had a son, Thomas, in 1615. The next year she travelled to England, where she died in 1617.

b
What are days for?

Days are where we live.

They come, they wake us.

Time and time over.

They are to be happy in:

Where can we live but days?

c
IN THE WORLD OF DISNEYLAND the whole family can enjoy playing in the home of their favourite Disney friends. There is a wide selection of popular and more unusual gifts available at the Disney shops. Well worth a visit, too, are the mountains, beaches, deserts and forests.

d
PYRAMID (n) 1. Monumental (esp. ancient Egyptian) structure of stone. 2. Solid of this shape with base of 3 or more sides. PYRAMIDIST (n) Student of structure and history of Egyptian pyramids.

e
CENTIPEDES have many body sections. Each body section has one pair of legs. Millipedes have many body sections. Each body section has 2 pairs of legs. Spiders have 2 body sections and 4 pairs of legs.

f
Annie lived in Switzerland. It is a beautiful country: there are green fields and high mountains. Annie lived in a village in the hills. One day, Annie took her sheep to the fields. She saw something strange.

g
Doctor, Doctor! My child has eaten my pen!
OK, I'm coming.
Doctor, what can I do until you arrive?
Use a pencil!

2 At the library

▶ *Where can you find these books in the library?*
Write the name of the section in the library under each title.

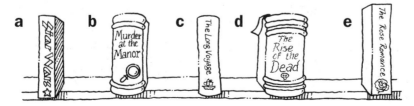

a   **b**   **c**   **d**   **e**

_____   _____   _____   _____   _____

Written by Pilar Cuder Domínguez, Raquel Rodríguez Tuñas
© David Spencer, David Vaughan 1996 Published by Heinemann English Language Teaching

1 *Let's go together!*

Activity	_____
Day	_____
Time	_____

go cycling

go to the cinema

go to the school disco

go to the swimming pool

go to a party

7 pm   8 pm   9 pm

FRIDAY   SATURDAY   SUNDAY

2 *Come to my party!*

Student A

Ring your friend.

Say hello and your name.

Say when you are going to have a party and invite your friend.

Tell your friend the time the party starts.

Say you are looking forward to seeing your friend.

Say goodbye.

Student B

Answer the phone.

Say hello.

Accept your friend's invitation. Ask what time.

Thank your friend for the invitation.

Say goodbye.

Written by Pilar Cuder Domínguez, Raquel Rodríguez Tuñas
© David Spencer, David Vaughan 1996 Published by Heinemann English Language Teaching

1 Let's go together!

Activity	(R) Talking about plans
Language	Going to
Interaction	Mingle (half class)
Time	15 minutes

1 Make a copy of the worksheet for each student.

2 Ask them to fill in the box selecting an activity, a day and a time from the ones given.

3 Explain to the students that they have to find other students who are going to do the same activity at the same time and on the same day, by asking and answering questions.

4 Separate the class into two groups and send them to different parts of the classroom. Students ask and answer questions. When they find someone who is doing the same activity on the same day at the same time, they say 'Let's go together!' and link arms. They continue to look for more people to join them.

Example:
A: *Are you going to go to the swimming pool?*
B: *Yes, I am. On Friday.*
A: *What time are you going to go?*
B: *At seven o'clock.*
A: *Me too! Let's go together!*

5 At the end, some groups can report to the whole class about where they're going, what day, what time and who with.

2 Come to my party!

Activity	(R) Invitations
Language	Going to
Interaction	Pairs
Time	10 minutes

1 Make one copy of the material for each pair.

2 Ask students to get into pairs. Give out the worksheets and ask students to look at their part.

3 Students follow the cues in their worksheets to have the phone conversation. Before they start, make sure they know what they are going to say.

4 Ask students to change roles. This time A students should refuse the invitation, giving a reason, and B students should say they are sorry A students can't come. You may want to revise ways of making, accepting or refusing invitations.

3 *The party's over!*

	Me	My Partner
when/last go/party?	_____	_____
where/be?	_____	_____
what time/start?	_____	_____
what time/finish?	_____	_____
what/wear?	_____	_____
what/do?	_____	_____
many people?	_____	_____
what kind/music?	_____	_____
what/do/before party?	_____	_____
have/good time?	_____	_____

Written by Pilar Cuder Domínguez, Raquel Rodríguez Tuñas
© David Spencer, David Vaughan 1996 Published by Heinemann English Language Teaching

3 The party's over!

. . . .

Activity (E) Talking about parties

Language Past simple

Interaction Pairs

Time 20 minutes

1 Make a copy of the worksheet for each student.

2 Ask students to get into pairs. Students complete the 'Me' column without showing their partners.

3 Students complete the 'My partner' column by asking questions. You may want to practise some of the questions first.

Example:
Were there many people? or How many people went?
Did you have a good time?
Where was the party?

4 Students compare the different parties, and report to the class.

Example:
Jamie's last party started earlier, there were more people and they listened to rock music. At my party we listened to heavy metal and pop music. We both had a good time.
Note: A revision of comparatives might also be useful.

1 Would you like to ... ?

▶ *Look at Kate's face and write her reply to these invitations.*

1 Would you like to go to a concert?

I'm sorry, I can't. I have to study.

2 Would you like to go to the cinema?

_____

3 Do you want to come to a party?

_____

4 Do you want to go to the zoo?

_____

5 Would you like to visit the museum?

_____

6 Would you like to come to the school disco?

_____

7 Do you want to go cycling tomorrow?

_____

2 Mr Bossy's diary

▶ *Look at Mr Bossy's diary and tick (✓) the invitations he can accept.*

MONDAY 19
4 pm Meet Captain Smith

TUESDAY 20
1 pm Lunch with Mr Hope

WEDNESDAY 21

THURSDAY 22
2 pm Play tennis

FRIDAY 23
8 am Travel to Paris

Aileen and Thomas Hartley
request the honour of your presence at the
marriage of their daughter Elizabeth to Vincent Green
on Wednesday, 21st December at 12:00 pm
at St Mary's Church, Bolton

The Scientists' Club
is hosting a luncheon
in honour of the Nobel Prize
winner Dr Knowall
at the Blue Hall, St John's College
on Monday 19th,
at 12:30 pm
R.S.V.P.

Dear Peter,
We are going to
have a Christmas
party at the office
on Friday 23rd. Can
you come? 6 o'clock
sharp! Bring a
bottle.

Now write what Mr Bossy is going to do on these dates:

1 On Monday 19th he _____

2 On Tuesday 20th he _____

3 On Wednesday 21st he _____

4 On Thursday 22nd he _____

5 On Friday 23rd he _____

1 The gunpowder plot

▶ **A** *Match the pictures and the dates. You can read the text about Guy Fawkes on page 46 of the textbook again.*

a November 5th 1605
b End of October 1605
c April–September 1604
d April 1604
e May 1605
f November 4th 1605

▶ **B** *Now write sentences explaining the pictures. Don't forget the dates.*

1 _____

2 _____

3 _____

4 _____

5 _____

6 _____

Written by Pilar Cuder Domínguez, Raquel Rodríguez Tuñas
© David Spencer, David Vaughan 1996 Published by Heinemann English Language Teaching

1 *I think you will!*

	Me	My Partner
Travel to distant places	_____	_____
Work with people	_____	_____
Have an unusual pet	_____	_____
Win a competition	_____	_____
Do a lot of sport	_____	_____
Be rich	_____	_____
BE FAMOUS	_____	_____
Have children	_____	_____
Learn another language	_____	_____
Work with machines	_____	_____
Meet a lot of people	_____	_____
Live in a foreign country	_____	_____
Go to university	_____	_____
Move to a different town or city	_____	_____
Get married	_____	_____

How well do you **really** know your partner? Check your score!

3 = You know your partner quite well.

4 = You know your partner very well.

5–6 = You know your partner extremely well.

0 = You don't know your partner at all.

1 = You know you partner very little.

2 = You don't know your partner very well.

Written by Pilar Cuder Domínguez, Raquel Rodríguez Tuñas
© David Spencer, David Vaughan 1996 Published by Heinemann English Language Teaching

1 I think you will!

· ·

Activity   **(R) Predictions**

Language   ***Will***

Interaction **Pairs**

Time   **15 minutes**

1 Make one copy of the worksheet for each student. Ask students to get into pairs.

2 Students should complete the column headed 'Me' by ticking six things they think they will do in the future.

3 The purpose of the activity is to guess their partner's future activities. Students fill in the column headed 'My Partner' by ticking the six things they think their partner will do in the future.

4 To find out how well they know their partner, they take turns to ask and answer questions about the six activities they have predicted for their partner's future life.

Example:
Will you live in a different country?
Will you meet a lot of people?

5 Finally, students check their scores. Ask some students to report surprising, interesting or unusual things they have found out to the class.

② *Perfect world!*

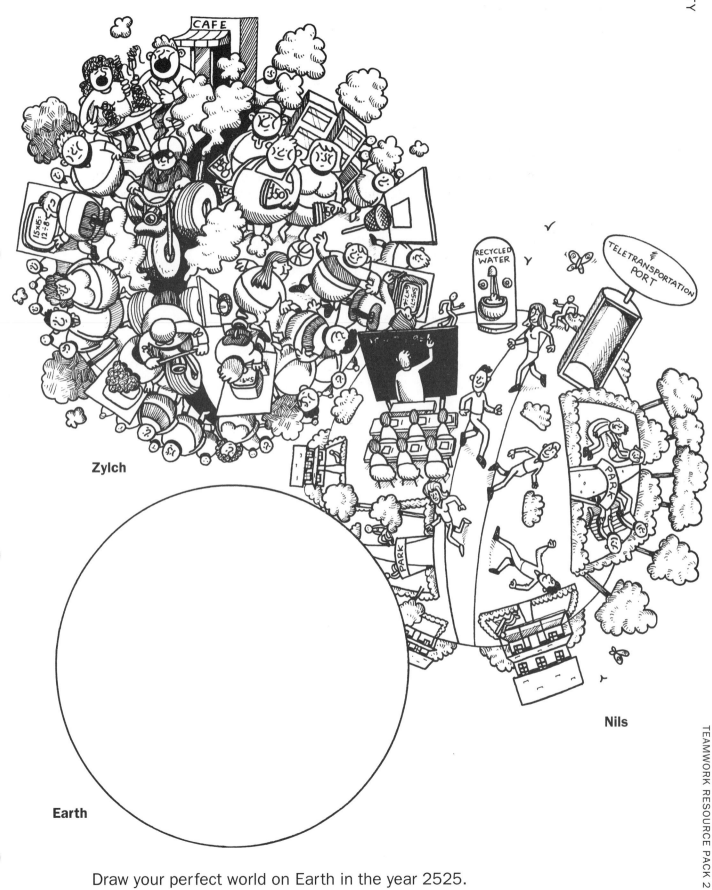

Zylch

Nils

Earth

Draw your perfect world on Earth in the year 2525.

Written by Pilar Cuder Domínguez, Raquel Rodríguez Tuñas
© David Spencer, David Vaughan 1996 Published by Heinemann English Language Teaching

2 Perfect world!

· ·

Activity   **(E) Predictions**

Language   *Will*

Interaction **Pairs; groups of 4**

Time   **25 minutes**

1 Make one copy of the worksheet for each pair. Ask students to get into pairs.

2 Each pair looks at the planets and decides what they like about that future life.

    Example:
    In the year 2525 people on planet Zylch will be very rich.
    In the year 2525 there won't be any pollution on Nils.

3 They draw a picture of their ideal future on Earth inside the planet provided.

4 Ask students to join up with another pair to make groups of four. The pairs explain their ideal planets to each other.

5 In their groups of four they agree on the six features of their ideal future and draw a poster to present them to the rest of the class.

6 If you like, you can organize a classroom display of their posters around the walls.

1 How do you feel?

▶ *How do you feel in these situations? Tick (✔) the corresponding adjectives in each case. You can tick more than one.*

	interested	patient	sad	bored	tired	worried	excited
You listen to your best friend's problems							
You have to do jobs at home							
You take an exam							
You receive an invitation							
You win a competition							
You are late for school							
You forget to do something important							

2 Robot time

▶ **A** *Look at this robot and predict what things or jobs it will do. Tick (✔) the right boxes.*

CDR-300 will ...

- [ ] drive you to school
- [ ] do the housework
- [ ] talk to people
- [ ] help you do your homework
- [ ] answer your letters
- [ ] help you pass English exams
- [ ] take messages

▶ **B** *Now make sentences.*

CDR-300 will ...   CDR-300 won't ...

TEAMWORK RESOURCE PACK 2

Written by Pilar Cuder Domínguez, Raquel Rodríguez Tuñas
© David Spencer, David Vaughan 1996 Published by Heinemann English Language Teaching

1 Into the future

▶ **A** *Scientists say that our homes will be like this in the year 2233. Look at the picture and complete the sentences.*

1 People _____ on water beds.

2 People _____. Their computers will produce their food.

3 Children _____ to school. They will study at home.

4 People _____ robot pets.

5 Doors _____ automatically.

6 Cars _____ electricity, so there _____ any pollution.

7 There _____ solar energy.

8 Robots _____ housework.

9 People _____ a gym at home.

▶ **B** *Do you like this home? Choose the three best things and write your reasons.*

Written by Pilar Cuder Domínguez, Raquel Rodríguez Tuñas
© David Spencer, David Vaughan 1996 Published by Heinemann English Language Teaching

1 *Shopping time*

Student A

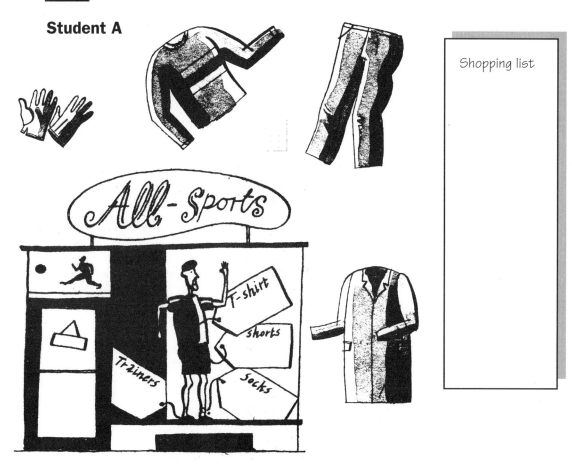

Shopping list

✂ -

Student B

Shopping list

Written by Pilar Cuder Domínguez, Raquel Rodríguez Tuñas
© David Spencer, David Vaughan 1996 Published by Heinemann English Language Teaching

Photocopiable **55**

1 Shopping time

· ·

Activity   **(R) Roleplay of a shopping dialogue**

Language   **Talking about colour, price and size**

Interaction **Pairs**

Time   **10 minutes**

1 Make one copy of the student A and student B material for each pair.

2 Ask students to get into pairs. Ask them to divide the worksheet into student A and student B.

3 Students A and B complete the label for each item in their shop window with the price, colour and size.

4 Then each student writes their own shopping list, choosing two of the items around the list and noting down the colour, size and price they would like.

5 Tell students they are now going to act out a dialogue. Student A is the shop assistant, student B is the customer. Student B should try to buy the items on his/her shopping list.

When they finish they change roles and student A is the customer and student B the shop assistant.

Example:
A: *Can I help you?*
B: *Yes, please. I'm looking for a jumper.*
A: *What size are you?*
B: *Medium.*
A: *I'm sorry, we've only got small.*
B: *OK, thank you. Goodbye.*

6 Some pairs act out a conversation for everyone in the class to hear.

2 *Guess what!*

▶ *Guess the object your group leader is holding. You can only ask questions which answer with* yes *or* no.

Written by Pilar Cuder Domínguez, Raquel Rodríguez Tuñas
© David Spencer, David Vaughan 1996 Published by Heinemann English Language Teaching

Photocopiable

2 Guess what!

·····················

Activity   (E) Talking about objects

Language   **Asking for information about shops, size, colour, price**

Interaction **Groups of 4**

Time   **20 minutes**

1 Make one copy of the set of cards for each group of four.

2 Ask students to get into groups of four and to cut out the cards and shuffle them. They put the pack of cards face down on the table.

3 Explain that the aim of the activity is to collect as many objects as possible. To do this they have to ask *yes/no* questions in order to guess the objects.

4 On the board write Shop? Home? Use? Colour? Size? Price?
Elicit possible *yes/no* questions for each.

Example:
Shop?   *Did you buy it in a ... (clothes shop)? Can you buy it in a ... (supermarket)?*
Home?   *Is this object usually in the home? Do you use this object at home?*
Use?   *Do you use it? Can you ... (read) it? Can you ... (eat) it?*
Colour?   *Is it ... (red)? Is it one colour?*
Size?   *Is it big? Is it smaller than a ... ?*
Price?   *Is it cheap? Is it more expensive than a ... ?*

5 The dealer picks up the first card, without showing it to the rest of the group, and answers *yes* or *no* to the questions the other students ask.

6 When students think they know the answer, they ask: *Is the object a ... ?*
If they are correct then they keep the card and the student to the right of the dealer picks up the next card. If they are not correct, then the other students in the group continue to ask questions until someone guesses the object.

7 When there are no cards left, students count how many they have got. The person with the most cards is the winner.

1 Shopping list

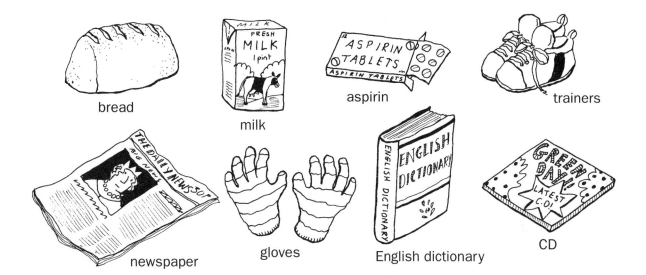

bread

milk

aspirin

trainers

newspaper

gloves

English dictionary

CD

▶ *You want to buy the items above. Draw your route on the map and then complete the text.*

START

First, I think I'll go to the _____ and buy

_____. Next, I'll buy _____

at the _____. Then, I'll go to the

_____ for _____.

After that, I'll buy _____ at the

_____. Later, I'll get _____ at

the _____, and _____ at the

_____. Finally, I'll buy _____ at

the _____ and _____

at the _____.

Written by Pilar Cuder Domínguez, Raquel Rodríguez Tuñas
© David Spencer, David Vaughan 1996 Published by Heinemann English Language Teaching

TEAMWORK RESOURCE PACK 2

1 Empty pockets

▶ **A** *Fill in this police report with information from page 60 of your Student's Book.*

Name: _____

Age: _____

Lost item: _____

When: _____

Where: _____

How it happened: _____

_____

_____

▶ **B** *You are Richard. Your father found the money. Write a letter to the police, explaining what happened. End your letter by saying you are sorry for the trouble you caused.*

Written by Pilar Cuder Domínguez, Raquel Rodríguez Tuñas
© David Spencer, David Vaughan 1996 Published by Heinemann English Language Teaching

1. *Which way?*

Student A

Student B

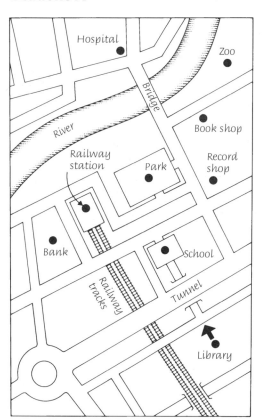

I left the library and went through the tunnel into the school. I walked out of the school, over the railway bridge, went right round the railway station, through the park, and over the bridge. Where did I go?

2 *Sydney-Perth rally*

Written by Pilar Cuder Domínguez, Raquel Rodríguez Tuñas
© David Spencer, David Vaughan 1996 Published by Heinemann English Language Teaching

1 Which way?

Activity (R) Understanding directions

Language Prepositions of movement

Interaction Groups of 4

Time 15 minutes

1 Make copies of the material for each pair.

2 Ask students to get into pairs. They divide the worksheet into the student A and student B material.

3 Explain that in each pair student A has a map and student B has a description. The aim of the activity is for student A to find out where student B went.

4 Student B reads the text aloud while student A listens and draws the route on the map.

5 They check together, by comparing the map and the text.

2 Sydney-Perth rally

Activity (E) Giving and following directions

Language Prepositions of movement

Interaction Pairs

Time 15 minutes

1 Make a copy of the map for each student.

2 Ask students to get into pairs. Individually, they draw the route of their choice from Sydney to Perth. They should include at least six of the places/features on the way.

3 In pairs, student A describes the rally route through Australia, and student B draws the route on the map. Then they exchange roles, and student B describes the route while student A draws.

4 Finally they compare maps.

3 Aliens

Student A

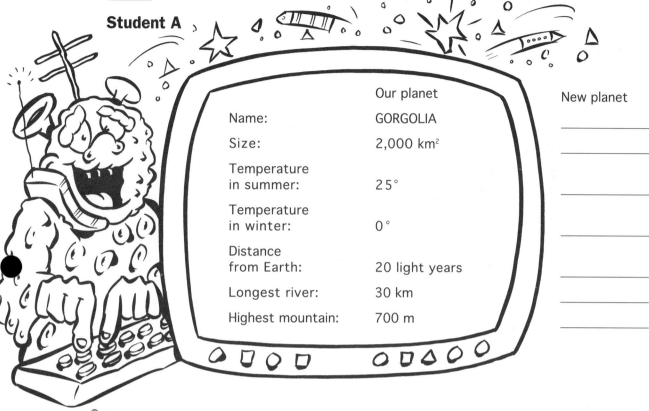

	Our planet	New planet
Name:	GORGOLIA	_____
Size:	2,000 km²	_____
Temperature in summer:	25°	_____
Temperature in winter:	0°	_____
Distance from Earth:	20 light years	_____
Longest river:	30 km	_____
Highest mountain:	700 m	_____

✂ -

Student B

	Our planet	New planet
Name:	MIR	_____
Size:	2,000,000 km²	_____
Temperature in summer:	32°	_____
Temperature in winter:	10°	_____
Distance from Earth:	30 light years	_____
Longest river:	700 km	_____
Highest mountain:	3,600 m	_____

Written by Pilar Cuder Domínguez, Raquel Rodríguez Tuñas
© David Spencer, David Vaughan 1996 Published by Heinemann English Language Teaching

3 Aliens
• • • • • • • • • • •

Activity   (E) Giving factual information

Language   How + adjective

Interaction Pairs

Time   15 minutes

1 Make one copy of the worksheet for each pair.

2 Ask students to get into pairs and to divide the worksheet into material for student A and student B.

3 Tell students they are aliens from different planets who are making contact by mobile telephone. The aim of the activity is to exchange information about their planets. Make sure they understand they have to find out the same information about the other planet as they have for their own (name, size, temperature in summer and winter, how far it is from Earth, how long the longest river is and how high the tallest mountain is). If necessary, check that they know what questions to ask.

4 They take turns to ask and answer questions about the planets.

Example:
A: *What's the name of your planet?*
B: *Mir.*
A: *How big is Mir?*
B: *It's two million square kilometres.*

1 Tell me how...

▶ *Complete each sentence with the correct adjective from the box.*

a How _____tall_____ is your brother?   1.85 m

b How _____ is Everest?   8,848 m

c How _____ is a Mercedes?   230 km/h

d How _____ is the Nile?   6,700 km

e How _____ is Scotland from London?   450 km

f How _____ is Seville in summer?   42°C

g How _____ is Alaska in winter?   –30°C

~~tall~~	far	~~cold~~	long	fast	hot	**high**

2 Good, better and the best!

▶ *Complete the sentences with the right form of the adjective in brackets.*

a I think Velázquez is _____ than Picasso, but Miró is
the _____. (good)

b A washing machine is _____ than a bike, but a
computer is the _____. (expensive)

c Michael Jordan is _____ than Magic Johnson, but
Shaquille O'Neill is the _____.(tall)

d A book is _____ than a film, but a computer
game is the _____. (interesting)

e A shark is _____ than a dolphin, but a whale is the
_____. (heavy)

f A hurricane is _____ than a storm, but a typhoon is
the _____. (bad)

Written by Pilar Cuder Domínguez, Raquel Rodríguez Tuñas
© David Spencer, David Vaughan 1996 Published by Heinemann English Language Teaching

1 Text maze

· · · · · · · · · · · · · · · · ·

▶ *Here are sentences from two different texts. Decide which of the sentences correspond to each picture and then put them in order. Write the letters in the correct order inside the pictures.*

a | The inventor WK Kellogg worked in a hospital in Michigan, USA.

b | The drink was not very popular at first.

c | However, many patients didn't enjoy eating corn.

d | JS Pemberton was a doctor.

e | Soon, everybody wanted to eat them!

f | Pemberton mixed cola nuts with carbonated water and he called his drink Coca-Cola.

g | That was why, in 1894, Mr Kellogg created Cornflakes, a more tasty way to eat cereals.

h | Now, it is a very popular drink and the company is one of the biggest in the USA.

i | Many of his patients had stomach problems and headaches so in 1886 he created a new drink.

j | He helped his patients with exercise and a special diet, including cereals such as corn or wheat.

Cornflakes

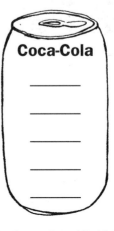
Coca-Cola

Written by Pilar Cuder Domínguez, Raquel Rodríguez Tuñas
© David Spencer, David Vaughan 1996 Published by Heinemann English Language Teaching

1 *Find someone who ...*

Name: _____

Name: _____

Name: _____

Name: _____

Name: _____

Name: _____

Name: _____

Name: _____

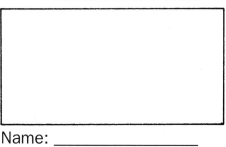

Name: _____

Name: _____

Name: _____

Name: _____

1 Find someone who ...

Activity (R) Talking about experiences

Language Present perfect

Interaction Mingle (2 mini-mingles)

Time 20 minutes

1 Make one copy of the worksheet for each student. Hand them out and ask the students to fill in the last two boxes with two more activities.

2 The aim is to find a different person for each activity. Explain that when a picture is crossed out, it means *never*, and they need to find someone who answers *no*.

3 Divide the class into two groups and send them to opposite ends of the classroom.

4 Students look at the pictures and think about the questions they will ask. They must think of two more experiences to ask other students about.

5 Students ask one another the questions and complete the 'Name' sections.

Example:
A: *Have you ever climbed a tree?*
B: *Yes, I have. (A writes B's name in the appropriate space.)*
A: *Have you ever been to Paris?*
C: *Yes, I have.*
A: *Have you ever been to Paris?*
D: *No, I haven't. (A writes D's name in the appropriate space.)*

6 Ask some students to report to the rest of the class.

2 *Around the world*

Student A

✂ -

Student B

TEAMWORK RESOURCE PACK 2

Written by Pilar Cuder Domínguez, Raquel Rodríguez Tuñas
© David Spencer, David Vaughan 1996 Published by Heinemann English Language Teaching

2 Around the world

....

Activity   **(R) Talking about experiences**

Language   **Present perfect**

Interaction **Pairs**

Time   **15 minutes**

Materials **Scissors (optional)**

1 Make one copy of the worksheet for each pair.

2 Ask students to get into pairs and hand out the student A and student B material.

3 Individually, students choose four of the pictures for their photo album. They cut or tear them out and put them in the corresponding spaces in the photo album (or they can glue them into the photo album), without showing their album to their partner.

4 In pairs, students guess where their partners have been by asking *yes/no* questions. If necessary, you can ask students for names of countries and write a list on the blackboard, before they start.

Example
A: *Have you been to Scotland?*
B: *Yes, I have. Have you been to India?*
A: *No, I haven't. Have you been to France?*
B: *No, I haven't.*

If they have problems guessing one of the places, they can ask for clues.

5 When they have guessed all the countries, they show each other their albums.

6 Some students report to the class about where their partner has been.

3 *Indiana's back!*

Student A

HOW MANY EXPEDITIONS?

TRAVEL ALONG THE NILE?

EXPLORE A PYRAMID?

DISCOVER A LOST CITY?

FIND ANY TREASURE?

PARACHUTE?

GO TO THE JUNGLE?

GO TO THE NORTH POLE?

HOW MANY FILMS?

HOW MANY BOOKS?

Student B

21 March

I've parachuted for the first time. It was very easy!

1 April

Today I've seen huge crocodiles on the banks of the Nile. But I didn't go to see the pyramids because I wasn't feeling well after I saw the crocodiles.

15 May

I've reached the North Pole on foot. It's not that cold here !!!

3 July

I've found the lost city of Pombal! It wasn't difficult. I was looking for my dog when I saw a strange building in the jungle. But there wasn't any gold.

29 August

I'm incredible! This is my 16th expedition!!! I think I'm going to write my 11th book. And I'll never have Madonna in my films again. I didn't like her in my 6th film, she's too old.

Written by Pilar Cuder Domínguez, Raquel Rodríguez Tuñas
© David Spencer, David Vaughan 1996 Published by Heinemann English Language Teaching

3 Indiana's back!

• •

Activity   **(E) Talking about experiences**

Language   **Present perfect**

Interaction **Pairs**

Time   **20 minutes**

1 Make one copy of the worksheet for each pair.

2 Ask students to get into pairs and hand out the student A and student B material.

3 Explain that student A is a reporter who is going to interview the famous explorer Indiana (student B).

4 Student A prepares the questions while student B reads the diary.

5 Then student A interviews student B, who answers according to the information in the diary.

Written by Pilar Cuder Domínguez, Raquel Rodríguez Tuñas
© David Spencer, David Vaughan 1996 Published by Heinemann English Language Teaching

1 Word jungle

▶ Find ten past participles in the word puzzle and write them next to the corresponding infinitive. The past participles go

```
A F H E A R D R P N
W O A R S T R B C E
R L M A W E I R H K
E L M F U N E E B A
N O A T M T R N R T
S W F O U D R P B C
K E L D N I T U V R
T D R U C W O T E S
W A O D E L L I K Y
I F H A D R W D S T
```

Infinitive	Past participle		Infinitive	Past participle
a take	_taken_		f find	_____
b follow	_____		g swim	_____
c have	_____		h hear	_____
d be	_____		i kill	_____
e see	_____		j put	_____

2 In the jungle

▶ Use the correct form of the verbs from **Word jungle** to complete these sentences.

a I have _____ the knife in my pocket.

b My friend has _____ a fever.

c We have _____ the river for two kilometres.

d I have _____ in the sea.

e We have _____ crocodiles.

f He has _____ the helicopter engine.

g I have _____ a snake with my knife.

h I have _____ a place where there is water.

i We have _____ hungry.

j The helicopter has _____ us out of the jungle.

Written by Pilar Cuder Domínguez, Raquel Rodríguez Tuñas
© David Spencer, David Vaughan 1996 Published by Heinemann English Language Teaching

Photocopiable **73**

1 To the Olympics

▶ *You are reporting the itinerary of the Olympic torch bearer.*
Complete each sentence with one of the words in the box below.

| through | *off* | **into** | ~~across~~ | onto | **down** |

a She's running _____ *across* _____ the street.

b She's going _____ the steps of the harbour.

c She's climbing _____ a boat.

d She's getting _____ the boat.

e She's running _____ the park.

f She's going _____ the Olympic stadium.

Written by Pilar Cuder Domínguez, Raquel Rodríguez Tuñas
© David Spencer, David Vaughan 1996 Published by Heinemann English Language Teaching

1 Showing off!

1 climb — EVEREST

2 climb — KILIMANJARO

3 climb — MONT BLANC

1 buy — Ferrari

2 buy — Porsche

3 buy — Twingo

1 go to — DISNEYLAND

2 go to — WATERPARK

3 go to — EURODISNEY

1 explore — The Amazon

2 explore — a jungle

3 explore — a forest

1 read — DON QUIXOTE

2 read — TREASURE ISLAND

3 read — Hello!

Written by Pilar Cuder Domínguez, Raquel Rodríguez Tuñas
© David Spencer, David Vaughan 1996 Published by Heinemann English Language Teaching

1 Showing off!

· · · · · · · · · · · · · · · · · · ·

Activity   **(R) Talking about experiences**

Language   **Present perfect**

Interaction **Groups of 3**

Time   **20 minutes**

1 Make copies of the set of cards for each group of three.

2 Ask students to make groups of three and cut out the cards.

3 One student shuffles the cards and deals them (five cards for each student). The student to his/her right places a card with a number 1 on the table and says the appropriate sentence; the student with the number 2 card of the same verb place his/her card on the table and says the sentence. Then the student with number 3 of the same verb places his/her card on the table and says the sentence and takes the three cards.

   Example:
   Student with card 1: *I've been to the water park.*
   Student with card 2: *I've been to Eurodisney.*
   Student with card 3: *I've been to Disneyland* (and picks up the cards).

4 The game continues like this until there are no more cards left. The winner is the student who gets the most cards.

2 *Have you ever ...?*

	Yes/no	When?	Where?	Other information
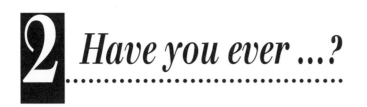 1 (travel/plane)?	_____	_____	_____	_____
2 (eat/Chinese food)?	_____	_____	_____	_____
3 (have/boy/girlfriend)?	_____	_____	_____	_____
4 (see/famous person)?	_____	_____	_____	_____
5 (visit/another country)?	_____	_____	_____	_____
6 (win/competition)?	_____	_____	_____	_____
7 (be/afraid)?	_____	_____	_____	_____
8 (sleep/tent)?	_____	_____	_____	_____

Now add two more questions of your own.

Written by Pilar Cuder Domínguez, Raquel Rodríguez Tuñas
© David Spencer, David Vaughan 1996 Published by Heinemann English Language Teaching

2 Have you ever ...?

Activity   **(E) Talking about experiences**

Language   **Present perfect**

Interaction **Pairs**

Time   **25 minutes**

1 Make one copy of the worksheet for each student.
2 Ask students to get into pairs and hand out the material.
3 Ask students to individually complete the last two questions with their own ideas.
4 Students take turns to ask questions and put a tick (✓) for *yes* and a cross (✗) for *no* under the correct column. Each student has to get more precise information about all the activities his/her partner has done. Encourage students to find out as much as possible. Demonstrate with one or two students before they do the activity.

Example
A: *Have you ever travelled by plane?*
B: *Yes, I have.*
A: *When was that?*
B: *Last summer.*
A: *Where did you go?/Who with?/Did you like it?*

5 Students can write a report about one or two of their partner's experiences, or tell the rest of the class any interesting information they have.

1 The latest news!

▶ **A** *Go back to page 81 in your Student Book. Are these statements TRUE or FALSE?*

1 Dory Dock is twelve years old. _____

2 She bought a dog for her mother. _____

3 Alexandra saw a shark yesterday. _____

4 Sharks never visit Britain. _____

5 Isabel Lord scored nine goals for her school football team. _____

6 Isabel wants to become a footballer. _____

7 People in Taplow don't like buying their milk in a supermarket. _____

8 Fred Bates is the village postman. _____

▶ **B** *These are some of the reporter's questions. Link the questions to the right people.*

a

1 Were you afraid?

2 Does your mother like animals?

3 Where do you study?

4 How old is the milkman?

5 What's the name of the pet shop?

6 Do you like swimming?

b

c

d

Written by Pilar Cuder Domínguez, Raquel Rodríguez Tuñas
© David Spencer, David Vaughan 1996 Published by Heinemann English Language Teaching

1 What a life!
·····················

▶ **A** *Think of one experience in your life for each category.*

1 The most exciting thing you've done in your life.

   *windsurfing*_____

2 The most boring thing you've done in your life.

   _____

3 The craziest thing you've done in your life.

   _____

4 The most dangerous thing you've done in your life.

   _____

5 The silliest thing you've done in your life.

   _____

▶ **B** *Now choose one of the activities you have written, illustrate
and write about it. Write it for a newspaper. Give as many details
as possible (when, where, how, why, who with, etc).*

ONLY 20p

THE DAILY TIMES

_____

_____

_____

_____

_____

_____

_____

_____

_____

Written by Pilar Cuder Domínguez, Raquel Rodríguez Tuñas
© David Spencer, David Vaughan 1996 Published by Heinemann English Language Teaching

1 *Crazy advice*

Problem	Solution	Solution
I have very little pocket money.	**I think you should rob a bank.**	You should go out with a rich boy/ girl.
I spend all my life doing housework.	**You should write to your fairy godmother.**	**I think you should buy a robot.**
My boy/ girlfriend doesn't love me.	**You should buy a different deodorant.**	**You should look for another boy/girlfriend.**
My sister takes my favourite CDs.	*I think you should lock your room.*	**You should give her your old CDs.**
My best friend tells my secrets to other people.	**I think you should tell him/her lies.**	You should tell his/her secrets to other people.
My parents say I can't go to the disco on Saturday night.	**You should promise to come home before twelve o'clock.**	You should invite all your friends to your house.

Written by Pilar Cuder Domínguez, Raquel Rodríguez Tuñas
© David Spencer, David Vaughan 1996 Published by Heinemann English Language Teaching

Photocopiable   **81**

1 Crazy advice

· · · · · · · · · · · · · · · · · · · ·

Activity   **(R) Giving advice**

Language   ***Should***

Interaction **Mingle (half-class)**

Time   **20 minutes**

1 Make two copies of the set of cards.

2 Divide the class into two groups and send them to opposite ends of the classroom.

3 Cut out the cards and give each student one. In each group every problem should have two solutions. If the number of students does not divide by three, then make sure each problem has at least one solution. Explain to the students that each student with a problem should find two solutions, though some problems may only have one.

4 The students with the problem should walk around saying their problem aloud. The other students give them advice. When the student with the problem finds the 'adviser', they link arms. When they find the second solution, the group of three go to the front of the classroom. The activity ends when all the problems have been solved.

5 Each group then repeats the problem and the two solutions for everybody to hear.

6 Students suggest alternative solutions and the class votes on the best advice.

2 *Guess my job!*

Do you have to ...?	Name: _____	Name: _____
• wear a uniform	_____	_____
• work long hours	_____	_____
• work at the weekend	_____	_____
• work at night	_____	_____
• get up early	_____	_____
• travel long distances	_____	_____
• go to bed late	_____	_____
• wear special clothes	_____	_____
• have special abilities	_____	_____
• work indoors all the time	_____	_____
• have a special diet	_____	_____

3 *Can you believe it?*

Student A

Yesterday I was with my (1) _____ in (2) _____, and something incredible happened. (3) _____ was standing there. She started talking. She said: 'I'm a very (4) _____ person and I should go to Hollywood to make a (5) _____ film with (6) _____ and (7) _____'. Before she left she invited me to a party in (8) _____. I haven't got anything special to wear but my (9) _____, who is a (10) _____, will lend me his/her (11) _____. So I´ll go in style!

Student B

1) Animal: _____
2) Place: _____
3) Name of a famous actress: _____
4) Adjective to describe a person: _____
5) A type of film: _____
6) Name of a famous actor: _____
7) Name of a famous singer: _____
8) Place: _____
9) Member of family: _____
10) Job: _____
11) Item of clothing: _____

2 Guess my job!

• •

Activity   **(R) Talking about obligation**

Language   **Have to**

Interaction **Groups of 4**

Time   **20–25 minutes**

1 Make one copy of the worksheet for each student.
2 Ask students to get into groups of four. Each student thinks of a job and doesn't tell his/her groupmates.
3 In pairs, students take turns to ask and give information about their jobs. When the answer is affirmative, they tick (✓) the first column, or note any information.

Example:
A: *Do you have to wear a uniform?*
B: *Yes, I do.*
A: *(Ticks first column.) Do you have to work at the weekend?*
B: *Sometimes, but not always.*
A: *(Writes 'sometimes' in the first column.) And do you work at night?*
B: *No, I don't.*

4 When they finish, they exchange partners and take it in turns to give information about the job of the groupmate they have interviewed.

Example:
She has to wear a uniform. She sometimes works at the weekend, but she doesn't have to work at night.

5 Each student tries to guess the two jobs and writes them down.
6 Students comment on and compare their answers.

3 Can you believe it?

• •

Activity   **(E) Telling an anecdote**

Language   **Revision of items of clothing, adjectives, animals and jobs**

Interaction **Pairs**

Time   **10 minutes**

1 Make one copy of the material for each pair.
2 Ask students to get into pairs and divide the material into student A and student B.
3 Student A reads silently the text, while student B completes the chart with one word in each space. If necessary, check that they can remember names of members of a family, animals, items of clothing and adjectives.
4 Student A asks student B to call out a word, according to the number given. She or he then writes the word in the space in the story.
5 After all the spaces are filled in, they practise reading the completed story.
6 Students then read their stories aloud to the rest of the class.

1 Lazy Tom

▶ *Give advice to lazy Tom.*

2 Should, shouldn't, have to or has to?

▶ *Complete the sentences with the correct verb.*

1 You _____ eat so much chocolate.

2 Mary _____ work on Saturdays.

3 Students at St John's School _____ wear a uniform.

4 If you want to travel to China, you _____ have a visa.

5 I think you _____ work harder.

6 You _____ tell your secrets.

7 Cinderella _____ do all the housework.

8 You _____ speak to your parents when you have a problem.

9 An athlete _____ train every day.

10 In Britain you _____ drive on the left.

Written by Pilar Cuder Domínguez, Raquel Rodríguez Tuñas
© David Spencer, David Vaughan 1996 Published by Heinemann English Language Teaching

1 Famous tales

▶ **A** *Match the texts with the titles.*

1 Sleeping Beauty
2 The Three Little Pigs
3 Pinocchio
4 Little Red Riding Hood
5 The Emperor's New Clothes

a
One by one, the crowd realised that the person to either side could no more see the new clothes than they could. 'Can you see them?' 'Of course, I can't. Do you think I'm stupid?' 'He is naked!' they shouted.

b
As soon as he told this lie, his nose grew two inches longer! Then he told another lie – and his nose grew longer still and went on growing.

c
The princess shall indeed grow in grace and beauty, but before the sun sets on her sixteenth birthday, she shall prick her finger on the spindle of a spinning wheel … and die.

d
'Oh, grandmother, what big ears you have!' 'The better to hear with,' was the reply. 'And what big eyes you have!' 'The better to see you with.' 'And what big hands you have!' 'The better to touch you with!' 'But, grandmother, what big teeth you have!' 'The better to eat you with!'

e
'A little pig will make a good lunch for me'. The wolf called, 'Little pig, little pig, let me come in.' 'Not by the hair of my chinny chin, chin!' said the first little pig. 'Then I'll huff and I'll puff and blow your house in!'

▶ **B** *Now give some advice to Sleeping Beauty, The Three Little Pigs, Pinocchio, Little Red Riding Hood and the Emperor.*

1 _____

2 _____

3 _____

4 _____

5 _____

1 *Find someone who is going to ...*

Name

... stay at home. _____

... go to a summer camp. _____

... visit another country. _____

... travel by plane. _____

... go to the seaside. _____

... study for exams in September. _____

... go to the mountains. _____

... go to a different school next year. _____

2 *Evaluating the course*

	Me	My Partner
The most interesting unit:	_____	_____
The most attractive topic:	_____	_____
The most amusing activity:	_____	_____
The most boring task:	_____	_____
The most exciting project:	_____	_____
The most difficult activity:	_____	_____
The easiest activity:	_____	_____
The best game:	_____	_____

Written by Pilar Cuder Domínguez, Raquel Rodríguez Tuñas
© David Spencer, David Vaughan 1996 Published by Heinemann English Language Teaching

1 Find someone who is going to ...

Activity   (R) Talking about summer holidays

Language   *Going to*

Interaction Mingle

Time   25 minutes

1 Make a copy of the worksheet for each student.

2 The aim is to find classmates who answer *yes* to the questions and write their names on the corresponding line. They should find a different person for each activity. If the group is very large, make two smaller groups and send them to different parts of the classroom.

3 Make sure students can form the questions correctly. If necessary, ask students what question they need to ask with each picture.

4 When students have finished, ask questions to find out what activities are the most common.

Example:
Who is going to go to the mountains?

Students raise their hands.

2 Evaluating the course

Activity   (R) Giving opinions

Language   Superlatives

Interaction Pairs

Time   20–25 minutes

1 Make a copy of the worksheet for each student.

2 Ask students to get into pairs.

3 First, each student fills in the 'Me' column, and then, in pairs, they take turns to ask questions and fill in the 'My partner' column. Make sure they know what question to ask.

Example:
Which do you think is ... (the most interesting unit)?
In your opinion, which is ... (the most attractive topic)?

4 Students comment on and compare their answers.

3. *Star system*

Interviewer:	Our next guest is one of Britain's biggest film stars. Please give a warm welcome to Emma Johnson. Emma, I believe you've just arrived here after a long trip to Japan. How was it?
Emma:	It was really good. I love Japan. It's a beautiful country.
Interviewer:	
Emma:	No, my second. I've been to Japan twice now.
Interviewer:	
Emma:	Well, although they're different from Japanese films, people there really like them.
Interviewer:	
Emma:	It's called *Nine Months*. It's very funny.
Interviewer:	
Emma:	Next month, so don't miss it!
Interviewer:	
Emma:	We had a lot of fun together. Arnie's a wonderful actor and a really nice person.
Interviewer:	
Emma:	Actually, Arnie and I became good friends, so we're going to make another film together.
Interviewer:	
Emma:	No, not at all. A spy thriller.
Interviewer:	
Emma:	Eight.
Interviewer:	
Emma:	No, I haven't, I think it'll be a great experience. I'm very excited.
Interviewer:	Well, good luck Emma and thanks for coming.

Questions

What are you going to do next?	The other star of the film is Arnie Schwarz. What was it like working with him?
When is it out?	
How many films have you made?	Tell us something about your latest film, Emma.
Was this your first visit?	
Another comedy?	You've never made a spy thriller before, have you?
Are your films very popular there?	

Written by Pilar Cuder Domínguez, Raquel Rodríguez Tuñas
© David Spencer, David Vaughan 1996 Published by Heinemann English Language Teaching

3 Star system

· · · · · · · · · · · · · · · · · · ·

Activity   **(E) Reading a text to reconstruct a dialogue**

Language   Simple past; present perfect; *going to* and *will*

Interaction Groups of 4

Time   30 minutes

Materials   Scissors

1 Make one copy of the worksheet for each group.
2 Ask students to get into groups of four and to cut out the questions to the interview.
3 Ask them to put the interviewer's questions in the right place in the dialogue to reconstruct the interview.
4 Check the results with the whole class.
5 Each group writes a report about Emma Johnson.

Key:

Interviewer: Our next guest is one of Britain's biggest stars. Please give a warm welcome to Emma Johnson. Emma, I believe you've just arrived after a long trip to Japan. How was it?

Emma: It was really good. I love Japan. It's a beautiful country.

Interviewer: *Was this your first visit?*

Emma: No, my second. I've been to Japan twice now.

Interviewer: *Are your films very popular there?*

Emma: Well, although they're different from Japanese films, people really like them.

Interviewer: *Tell us something about your latest film, Emma.*

Emma: It's called *Nine Months*. It's very funny.

Interviewer: *When is it out?*

Emma: Next month, so don't miss it!

Interviewer: *The other star of the film is Arnie Schwarz. What was it like working with him?*

Emma: We had a lot of fun together. Arnie's a wonderful actor and a really nice person.

Interviewer: *What are you going to do next?*

Emma: Actually, Arnie and I became good friends, so we're going to make another film together.

Interviewer: *Another comedy?*

Emma: No, not at all. A spy thriller.

Interviewer: *How many films have you made?*

Emma: Eight.

Interviewer: *You've never made a spy thriller before, have you?*

Emma: No, I haven't, I think it'll be a great experience. I'm very excited.

Interviewer: Well, good luck Emma and thanks for coming.

1 Letter to a penfriend

▶ **A** *Make notes about the topics below. Include three pieces of information in each one.*

1 Your likes and dislikes:

_____

_____

_____

2 Your daily routines:

_____

_____

_____

3 Your past experiences:

_____

_____

_____

4 Your future plans:

_____

_____

_____

▶ **B** *Now write a letter to a penfriend telling him/her about yourself and the topics mentioned above. Link the sentences with <u>and</u>, <u>after</u>, <u>when</u> or <u>because</u>.*

Written by Pilar Cuder Domínguez, Raquel Rodríguez Tuñas
© David Spencer, David Vaughan 1996 Published by Heinemann English Language Teaching

1 My advice

▶ **A** *What do you think is important to do in these areas?*

Grammar _____

_____

Vocabulary _____

_____

Reading _____

_____

Writing _____

_____

Speaking _____

_____

Listening _____

_____

Example:

Grammar I think you should use the Grammar Reference at the

back of the book. It's very useful to help you study.

▶ **B** *Write a letter to somone who is going to use this book next year and give him/her advice on how to study English.*

Written by Pilar Cuder Domínguez, Raquel Rodríguez Tuñas
© David Spencer, David Vaughan 1996 Published by Heinemann English Language Teaching

Revision Activities Key

UNIT 1

1 You name it!
a blackboard b desk c chalk
d ruler   e boardrubber
f dictionary g pencil h notebook

2 Welcome back!
A 1 d, 2 a, 3 e, 4 c, 5 b
B b   did, go, went
   c   Did he go, his, went, his
   d   did he do, travelled, swam
   e   did he come, came back

UNIT 2

1 As different as chalk and cheese
Answers may vary.

2 At the newsagent's
Answers may vary.

UNIT 3

1 What a life!
A once a week – yoga
   twice a week – fly long distances
   three or four times a week – photo
     sessions
   once a month – see parents
   not very often – go to restaurant
B Answers may vary.

2 Super models
Claudia is taller and more elegant than Cindy.
Cindy is shorter, thinner and more beautiful than Claudia.

UNIT 4

1 Goal!
a Peter usually gets up at seven.
b She goes swimming twice a week.
c She does judo every day.
d They often play football after school.
e My friends sometimes go to the sports club on Mondays.

2 To be or not to be ... fit!
Fit – eating fruit, running, dancing, walking to school
Unfit – eating hamburgers, watching TV, playing computer games, driving to school

UNIT 5

1 A letter from Egypt
door, lamp, bed, two statues, boxes, roses, table, plates, bread

2 A long time ago
Answers may vary.

UNIT 6

1 Story time
was sitting, was shining, were playing, was reading
saw, was wearing, was running, was holding
Answers may vary.

2 Interrogation
Answers may vary.

UNIT 7

1 Would you like to...?
Answers may vary.

2 Mr Bossy's diary
Tick wedding invitation and Scientists' Club's invitation.
1 's going to go to the luncheon at St John's College and he is going to meet Captain Smith.
2 's going to have lunch with Mr Hope.
3 's going to go to Elizabeth and Vincent's wedding.
4 's going to play tennis.
5 's going to travel to Paris.

UNIT 8

1 How do you feel?
Answers may vary.

2 Robot time
Answers may vary.

UNIT 9

1 Shopping list
Answers may vary.

UNIT 10

1 Tell me how...

b high   c fast   d long

e far   f hot   g cold

2 Good, better and the best!

a better, best   b more expensive, most expensive   c taller, tallest

d more interesting, most interesting

e heavier, heaviest   f worse, worst

UNIT 11

1 Word jungle

a take-taken, b follow-followed, c have-had, d be-been, e see-seen, f find-found, g swim-swum, h hear-heard, i kill-killed, j put-put.

2 In the jungle

a put   b had   c followed   d swum

e seen   f heard   g killed   h found

i been   j taken

UNIT 12

1 The latest news!

A 1 false   2 false   3 true

4 false   5 false   6 true

7 true   8 false

B 1 b, 2 a, 3 c, 4 d, 5 a, 6 b

UNIT 13

1 Lazy Tom

a He should tidy his bedroom./He should clean his bedroom.

b He should do the washing.

c He should make his bed.

d He should do the washing up./He should wash the dishes.

e He should do his homework.

2 Should, shouldn't, have to or has to?

1 shouldn't   2 has to   3 have to

4 have to   5 should   6 shouldn't

7 has to/shouldn't   8 should

9 has to   10 have to

UNIT 14

1 Letter to a penfriend

Answers may vary.

Extension Activities Key

UNIT 1

1 Check your spelling!
a poster b blackboard c boardrubber
d notebook e dictionary f chalk
g computer

2 Dear Peggy Sue
Britain, family, ferry, drove, sunny, didn't rain, swam, played volleyball, took

UNIT 2

1 Which section?
a horoscope b crossword c sport
d TV guide e film review f interview

2 Competition winner!
a Where and when were you born?
b What do you like? What don't you like?
c What are you hobbies?
d What is your favourite food/drink?
e Have you got any brothers and sisters?/
   Do you like being with your family?
f Have you got any pets?

UNIT 3

1 That's life!
A Advantages
   go to fantastic places
   wear beautiful clothes
   meet interesting people
   Disadvantages
   hard work
   not much time for friends and family
   not much time for hobbies
B Answers may vary.

UNIT 4

1 Game
Answers may vary.

2 Then and now
A 3, 4, 6, 9
B 1, 2, 5, 7, 8

UNIT 5

1 Egyptian adventure
1 d, 2 a, 3 e, 4 b, 5 c, 6 g, 7 f

2 Jumping knights
We opened the tomb and found the most incredible treasure in the heart of the pyramid.

UNIT 6

1 Book Puzzle
a Sixteenth-Century America
b Collected Poems
c Travel Guide to America
d The 'BEST' English Dictionary
e The Natural World
f Annie's Adventures
g The Book of Jokes

2 At the library
a Science fiction
b Detective
c Adventure
d Horror
e Romance

UNIT 7

1 The gunpowder plot
A 1 d, 2 c, 3 e, 4 b, 5 f, 6 a
B 1 Guy Fawkes and four men planned to blow up Parliament in April 1604.
   2 Guy Fawkes and four men made a tunnel between April and September 1604.
   3 Guy Fawkes bought the gun powder in May 1605.
   4 Robert Cecil received an anonymous letter with the message 'Parliament in danger!' at the end of October 1605.
   5 Guy Fawkes was arrested on November 4th 1605.
   6 The King opened Parliament on November 5th 1605.

UNIT 8

1 Into the future
A 1 will sleep   2 won't cook
   3 won't go   4 will have
   5 will open   6 will use, won't be
   7 will be   8 will do
   9 will have
B Answers may vary.

UNIT 9

1 Empty pockets

A Name: Richard Kemp;
Age: 14;
Lost item: £90;
When: last Saturday;
Where: Olympic sports shop;
How it happened: he went to the sports shop to buy a bicycle but when he went to pay, his pockets were empty.

B Answers may vary.

UNIT 10

1 Text maze

Cornflakes   a j c g e
Coca-Cola   d i f b h

UNIT 11

1 To the Olympics

b down   c onto   d off   e through   f into

UNIT 12

1 What a life!

Answers may vary.

UNIT 13

1 Famous tales

A 1 c, 2 e, 3 b, 4 d, 5 a
B Answers may vary.

UNIT 14

1 My advice

Answers may vary.

Heinemann English Language Teaching
A division of Reed Educational and Professional Publishing Ltd
Halley Court, Jordan Hill, Oxford OX2 8EJ

OXFORD MADRID FLORENCE ATHENS PRAGUE SÃO PAULO MEXICO CITY CHICAGO PORTSMOUTH (NH) TOKYO SINGAPORE KUALA LUMPUR MELBOURNE AUCKLAND JOHANNESBURG IBADAN GABORONE

ISBN 0 435 25062 0

Written by Pilar Cuder Dominguez and Raquel Rodriguez Tuñas

Text © David Vaughan and David Spencer 1996

Design and illustration © Heinemann Publishers (Oxford) Ltd 1996

Illustration © Jacky Rough p8

First published 1996

Designed by **AMR** Limited, Basingstoke

Cover illustration by The Point

Illustrated by: Robin Chevalier pp55, 57, John Gilkes p61 (a), Teri Gower pp15, 19, 21, 41, 42, 57, 89, Madelaine Hardie pp59, 66, Gillian Hunt pp61 (b), 65, 75, Geoff Jones p33, Andrew Keylock pp63, 69, 85, Ed McLachlan pp7, 11, 13, Julian Mosedale pp17, 45, 49, 60, 83, 91, Andrew Peters pp3, 23, 25, 39, 51, 53, 54, 86, John Richardson p28, Jacky Rough p8, Jake Tebbit p37, Simon Turner pp67, 79, Andrew Warrington pp9, 29, 31, 34, 48, Shaun Williams pp5, 27, 35, 47, 59. 74, 87.

Printed and bound in Great Britain by Scotprint Limited

96 97 98 99 10 9 8 7 6 5 4 3 2 1